ABCmouse.com
Early Learning Academy

Writing:
Sentence Practice

ABCmouse.com *Early Learning Academy* is the award-winning digital learning program that covers math, reading, science, social studies, art, music, and more for kids ages 2 to 8.

With more than 10,000 individual Learning Activities and over 850 lessons across 10 levels, ABCmouse is a proven educational resource that is trusted by parents and teachers across the U.S. and around the world.

Go to
www.ABCmouse.com
to learn more.

ABC Mouse

ABCmouse.com

At-Home
LEARNING TIPS ☑

Dear Families,

The keys to successfully managing a "learn-at-home" situation are often related to time and space. Here are a few tips to ensure that you and your child are getting the most of your opportunities to learn at home.

Managing Time

☐ Establish a routine for your day. For example, plan to start "learning time" at the same time every day, and schedule consistent breaks for meals, exercise, and free time. Make that routine as similar to your child's school day as possible.

☐ Set goals for how much time to spend on each learning activity, such as reading silently for 20 minutes. Be sure to celebrate when goals are achieved.

☐ Plan ahead for when you need time for yourself. Explain when that will be, and help your child use a clock to know when that time is over.

☐ Include your child in planning out how to spend your time. Children are much more likely to stick with a plan when they had a part in deciding what it is.

Managing Space

☐ Identify one or more "learning spaces" around your home. Pick places that are as comfortable and distraction-free as possible.

☐ Use headphones to cancel out noise when it's not possible to create a distraction-free space.

☐ Collect containers such as shoeboxes or small cubbies to hold school items.

☐ Choose one area of the house to store school items when not in use. Having a dedicated place to "turn in" and "pick up" items helps keep things organized.

☐ Allow children to use outdoor spaces when possible. Outdoor spaces provide fresh air and can help lift moods. They can also provide fantastic learning opportunities themselves!

☐ Just like with the last note about time, include your child in planning out how to use your space, too.

—Team ABCmouse

Coloring

Four Types of Sentences

Color the picture for each type of sentence.

Asking

"Where did all those books come from?"

Exclaiming

"I've never seen so many books!"

Telling

"We're having a book drive."

Commanding

"Bring all your books to the front office."

Write the correct punctuation at the end of each sentence. Use a **.**, **?**, or **!**.

The car is on the bridge

Can you see the water

Look at that big fish

The bridge is very long

Do you want to go for a ride

Read the poem. Write the missing words. Color the picture.

Can _____ come out and play with _____ ?
   (us, you)   (me, I)

_____ can play beside the sea.
(They, We)

Let's ask Lin and let's ask Jim.

I'll ask _____ and you ask _____ !
     (her, she)   (him, me)

Let's bring pails and shovels, too.

_____ is red and _____ is blue!
(Its, Mine)   (yours, them)

Answer Key						
you	me	We	her	him	Mine	yours

Choose the correct mark to put at the end of each sentence.

1. I want to get up at 7 o'clock___   ? .

2. What time is it___   ? !

3. Is it time to eat lunch ___   ? .

4. It is time to swim ___   ? !

5. When can we play soccer___   ? !

Draw and color a picture for one of the sentences.

Look at the picture. Read the sentence. Write the missing word.
Use the word box to help you.

Word Box

cowboy	enjoys	noise	soil	coins

1. Roy put three _____ coins _____ in his piggy bank.

2. Lea _____ riding her bike!

3. She heard a loud _____ .

4. The _____ is riding a horse.

5. Troy put the plant in the _____ .

_____

Look at the picture. Read the sentence. Write the correct word.

1.

The baby is happy.   The babies are happy.

The babies are happy.

2.

The berry is sweet.   The berries are sweet.

_____

3.

The puppy is cute!   The puppies are cute!

_____

4.

The pony is running.   The ponies are running.

_____

Write the correct describing word in each sentence.
The first one is done for you.

① A ⬡ is harder than a 🛏 .

hard, harder

② A 🚌 is _____ than a 🛒 .

fast, faster

③ The 🧍 is _____ than the 👶 .

old, older

④ The 🌳 is _____ than the 🌸 .

tall, taller

⑤ The 🍦 is _____ than the 🍲 .

cold, colder

Look at the picture. Read the sentence. Write the correct word.

1. Can you help _____ **me** _____ clean up the paint?
(I, me, they)

2. _____ are a great team!
(They, Us, Them)

3. I will share a snack with _____ .
(me, him, us)

4. Will you play with _____ ?
(her, we, us)

5. _____ is my best friend!
(She, He, I)

Look at the pictures and the sentences. Choose the correct verb to write in each blank.

	1. The boys _ _ _ _ _ _ _ _ _ apples. eat, eats
	2. My sister _ _ _ _ _ _ _ _ _ milk. drink, drinks
	3. Jean _ _ _ _ _ _ _ _ _ beans in her garden. grow, grows
	4. Amir and Lisa _ _ _ _ _ _ _ _ _ carrots. like, likes
	5. Emma _ _ _ _ _ _ _ _ _ a peach to Mark. give, gives

Finish each sentence by writing the verb in the blank space.
Add the letters *ed* to show that it happened in the past.

1. He _____ up high.
   jump

2. She _____ her dad.
   help

3. He _____ for a rock.
   look

4. She _____ the ball.
   want

5. We _____ on the grass.
   walk

6. I _____ in the park.
   play

14

Choose the correct pronouns to write in the blanks.

1. The horse _____ rides is white. _____ is black.

   them, mine, he   them, mine, he

2. The people are happy to see _____ . _____ like our King.

   his, him, we   his, him, we

3. _____ wish the King would stay with _____ all the time.

   his, I, us   his, I, us

4. Please tell _____ when _____ will come back again.

   hers, me, he   hers, me, he

Write the verb that agrees with each subject in the blank.

1. The librarian _____ you find your books.
   (help, helps)

2. Amelia and Maria _____ out chapter books.
   (check, checks)

3. The brothers _____ a book about dinosaurs.
   (read, reads)

4. Brandon _____ a book he finished.
   (return, returns)

5. The library _____ at 5 o'clock.
   (close, closes)

Answer Key 1. helps 2. check
3. read 4. returns 5. closes

ABCmouse.com®
TM & © 2020 Age of Learning, Inc.

Write the correct verb at the end of each sentence.

	The rabbit _____ . hop hops	**The rabbits** _____ . hop hops
	The boy _____ . run runs	**The boys** _____ . run runs
	The girl _____ . walk walks	**The girls** _____ . walk walks
	The cat _____ . eat eats	**The cats** _____ . eat eats

Look at the picture. Read the sentence. Write the missing word. Use the words in the box to help you.

Word Box

This	this	That	that
These	these	Those	those

1.

   ## This
   _____ is my basketball.

2.

   I will keep _____ toy cars!

3.

   Let's keep _____ game.

4.

   _____ shirts are the best!

ABCmouse.com®
TM & © 2020 Age of Learning, Inc.

Sentence Writing
More and Less: Weight

Look at each object on the balance. Write more or less in the blank.

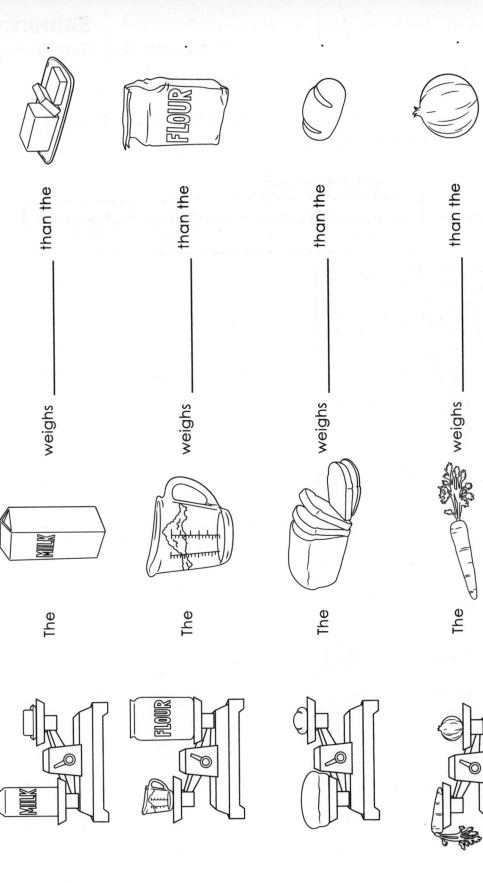

1. The _____ weighs _____ than the

2. The _____ weighs _____ than the

3. The _____ weighs _____ than the

4. The _____ weighs _____ than the

Read the sentence. Find a word that tells more about the person or an animal. Write the word. Draw a line before the -*er* or -*est* word ending.

1. The turtle is __slow/er__ than the rabbit.
   (slower, slowest)

2. The rabbit is _____ .
   (faster, fastest)

3. Lee has the _____ hair.
   (shorter, shortest)

4. Yan's hair is the _____ .
   (longer, longest)

5. The kitten is _____ than the dog.
   (smaller, smallest)

6. The dog is _____ than the kitten.
   (older, oldest)

Answer Key: 1. slow/er   2. fast/er   3. short/est   4. long/est   5. small/er   6. old/er

Read the poem. Write the missing words. Use the word box to help you.
Then color the picture.

Word Box

| house | cow | down | shout | mouse | town | now |

The wolf is gone. Let _____**town**_____ bells ring.

Jump up and _____ . Let's _____ and sing!

The pigs can leave their _____ right _____ .

And play with friends, the _____ and _____ !

Look at each picture and read the sentence that goes with it.
Write the correct word on the line, and color the picture.

1.

Last week, Carla and Tomas _____
(visits, visited, visiting)
the beach.

2.

Carla _____ a kite.
(flied, flew, fly)

3.

Tomas _____ in the sand.
(draw, drew, drawed)

4.

They _____ a picnic lunch.
(eats, ate, eated)

5.

Tomas _____ a crab walk by.
(watches, watcht, watched)

Answer Key 1. visited 2. flew 3. drew 4. ate 5. watched

Read the sentence. Look at the words below the line. Write the correct word.

1.

The turtle moves _____ in the grass.
(slow, slowly)

2.

The manatee is a _____ swimmer.
(graceful, grace)

3.

The great egret has a _____ yellow bill.
(point, pointy)

4.

Did the duck _____ behind the rock?
(disappear, appear)

5.

The alligator is an _____ animal.
(friendly, unfriendly)

Sentence Writing
Dinosaurs

Read each clue. Unscramble the letters. Write the word.
Draw and color a dinosaur.

Word Box

buried	roamed	huge	extinct	consumed

1. Long ago, dinosaurs _____ the earth.   deaorm

2. Fossils that are under the ground are _____ .   rubdie

3. Many dinosaurs _____ plants for food.   msoencud

4. No dinosaurs are alive today. They are _____ .   cnxiett

5. Some dinosaurs were small. Some were _____ .   geuh

Answer Key 1. roamed 2. buried 3. consumed 4. extinct 5. huge

Look at the picture. Read the sentence. Look at the words below the line. Write the correct spelling of the word in the blank.

1.

Mr. Wordsmith floats on a _____ in
(rast, raft, raff)
Hubert's pool.

2.

Hubert bought Mr. Wordsmith a new

_____ .
(vesk, vesp, vest)

3.

The brothers see a _____ .
(plane, blane, prane)

4.

There is a _____ in Mr. Wordsmith's
(skung, skuck, skunk)
garden.

5.

Hubert plays a song on his _____.
(trum, drum, prum)

Sentence Writing
Plurals Practice

Look at the picture. Read the sentence. Choose the correct word.
Write it on the line.

1. We like our new ___skates___!
(skates, skaties, skate)

2. There are three _____ in the basket.
(puppys, puppy, puppies)

3. The_____ are ripe and sweet.
(peachs, peaches, peach)

4. I will put five _____ in my piggy bank.
(pennies, penny, pennys)

5. Miguel set the _____ on the table.
(dish, dishs, dishes)

Look at the picture. Read the sentence. Choose the correct word. Write it.

1.  The __wolves__ look just like big dogs.
(wolf, wolves, wolfs)

2.  Please get off of my _____!
(foot, feet, foots)

3.  Rosa likes to brush Kona's _____!
(teeth, tooth, tooths)

4.  Pepper is chasing the _____!
(gooses, goose, geese)

5.  Otis is eating the _____ of bread.
(loaf, loaves, loafs)

Answer Key: 1. wolves 2. feet 3. teeth 4. geese 5. loaves

Read the sentence. Choose the correct word. Write it. Then color the picture.

1.

This is the _____ party hat.

(ducks, duck, duck's)

2.

These are the _____ presents.

(fish's, fish, fishes)

3.

This is the _____ gift bag.

(frog, frog's, frogs)

4.

This is the _____ balloon.

(turtle's, turtles, turtle)

Look at the picture. Read the sentence and write the missing word.

1.

This garden is _____ .
(yours, ours, hers)

2.

This watering can is _____ .
(theirs, mine, yours)

3.

That shovel is _____ .
(his, hers, ours)

4.

That garden is _____ .
(theirs, mine, yours)

Look at the picture. Choose the correct word to write in the blank.
Then color the picture.

1.

The puppy _____ the bow.
(ties, unties)

2.

The boy has a _____ of spaghetti.
(mouthful, mouth)

3.

The ice cream melted _____
(quick, quickly)

in the hot sun.

4.

The cat smells something _____ .
(fish, fishy)

5.

There was a rabbit in the hat, but the magician

made it _____ .
(appear, disappear)

Answer Key 1. unties **2.** mouthful **3.** quickly **4.** fishy **5.** disappear

Read each sentence about something that is happening now.
Then finish writing the sentence about what will happen in the future.
The first example is done for you.

1.

The dog is playing.

The dog _____ will play _____.

2.

They are floating.

They _____.

3.

The flowers are blooming.

The flowers _____.

4.

She is jumping.

She _____.

5.

The bird is singing.

The bird _____.

Look at the picture. Read the sentence. Choose a word to complete it. Write the word.

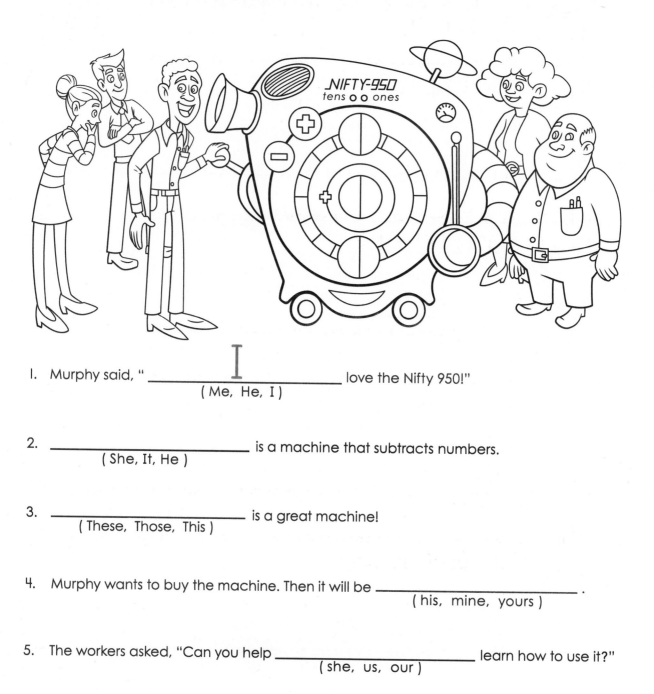

1. Murphy said, " _____ I _____ love the Nifty 950!"
(Me, He, I)

2. _____ is a machine that subtracts numbers.
(She, It, He)

3. _____ is a great machine!
(These, Those, This)

4. Murphy wants to buy the machine. Then it will be _____ .
(his, mine, yours)

5. The workers asked, "Can you help _____ learn how to use it?"
(she, us, our)

Write each sentence correctly. Be sure to start the sentence with a capital letter and end with a **.**, **?**, or **!**.

the dog runs

_____

fred reads a book

_____

did the girl walk

_____

you did well, Anna

_____

Sentence Writing
Sight Words: Grammar Kingdom

Choose a words from the word box to finish the sentences.
Then read the story.

Word Box

after	because	first	live	put	them	time

This is the _____ _____ the King

has come to the village. The people who _____

there are happy, _____ they want to

meet the King. They _____ on their best clothes.

_____ the King meets _____,

they will all have a big feast.

Look at the picture. Read the sentence. Write the missing word or words. Use the words in the box to help you.

Word Box

could   round   use   old

1. How _____ is Hugo today?

2. I wish I _____ live in a castle!

3. I will _____ a hose to water the garden.

4. The wheels on the bus go_____ and _____ !

Read the sentence. Write the missing word. Use the words in the box to help you. Then draw a picture of yourself walking on the moon!

Word Box

| your | very | were | their |

1. It was_____ exciting when the astronauts walked on the moon.

2. They wore_____ space suits.

3. The astronauts_____ brave!

4. When will you take_____ first trip into space?

Look at the picture. Read the sentence. Draw an "X" on the word that does not belong. Find the correct word in the box. Write it.

Word Box

people	feet	wolves	mice	children

1. The ~~child~~ eat ice cream cones. children

2. I have two foot! _____

3. The person are cheering. _____

4. The wolf are howling. _____

5. The mouse are eating cheese. _____

Read the sentence. Use fewer words to say the same thing. Add an apostrophe and an *s* to the noun. Color the pictures. The first one has been done for you.

1

This is the bat that belongs to the boy.

This is the boy's bat.

2

This is the glove that belongs to the catcher.

_____

3

This is the shirt that belongs to the girl.

_____

4

This is the helmet that belongs to the batter.

_____

Sentence Writing

Verbs: *-ing* and *-ed* endings

Read the sentences. Look at the two verbs below each line.
Write the verb with the correct ending in the sentence.

1. Last night, a spider _____ in my window.

   is jumping, jumped

2. It _____ now, so Jan is playing inside.

   is raining, rained

3. On Monday, I _____ to the park.

   is walking, walked

4. Sam _____ a game of tag right now.

   is playing, played

5. I _____ to my brother yesterday.

   is talking, talked

Look at the picture. Read the sentence. Write the missing word.
Use the Word Box to help you.

> fridge   bridge   lodge   ledge   badge

1.

The troll lived under an old _____ .

2.

The sheriff's _____ is shiny.

3.

I drank cocoa in the cozy_____ .

4.

Their _____ is like an art museum.

5.

A _____ is a good place to
nap—for a goat!

Draw a picture of yourself practicing one of these healthy habits. Write about the picture.

Healthy Habits

✓ Eating right

✓ Being active

✓ Getting plenty of sleep

✓ Keeping your body clean

Use one noun and one describing word from the word bank to finish each sentence. You can make silly sentences, if you want to. You do not have to use all the words in the word bank.

Nouns		Describing Words		
turkey	corn	yellow	tasty	sweet
salad	pie	green	fluffy	sleepy

The _____ is _____ .
noun   describing word

The _____ is _____ .
noun   describing word

The _____ is _____ .
noun   describing word

The _____ is _____ .
noun   describing word

Look at the picture. Read the sentence. Write the missing word.
Use the word box to help you.

Word Box *-ing*	Word Box *-ed*
floating kicking jumping	watched climbed pulled

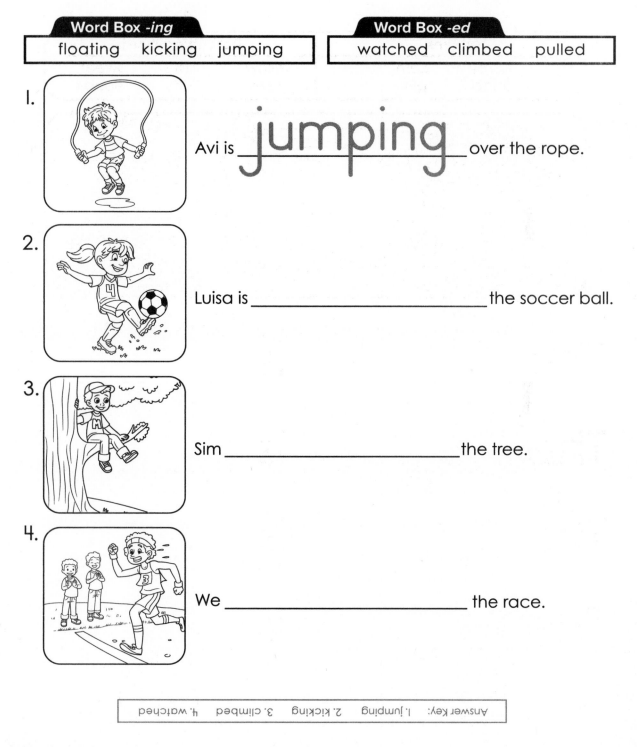

1. Avi is __jumping__ over the rope.

2. Luisa is _____ the soccer ball.

3. Sim _____ the tree.

4. We _____ the race.

Look at the picture. Read the sentence and write missing word.
Use the word box to help you.

apart	large	heart	party	March

1. Today is _____ 15th. It is Carly's birthday!

2. Her parents are throwing her a surprise _____ .

3. Carly swings and breaks _____ the piñata.

4. Carly gets a _____ necklace.

5. Her mom serves _____ slices of cake.

Write and Draw
Pasta Dish

Read the name of each food. Write another one you like. Choose foods for your pasta dish. Draw a picture of it. Write a sentence about it.

pasta   tomatoes   olives   peppers   meat balls   _____

Look at the picture. Read the first part of the sentence. Use the Sentence Parts Box to complete the sentence to make a compound sentence. Then color the picture.

but Austin had a flashlight.

but he wasn't sure what he'd find.

and it was marked with an *X*.

so he took it to the museum.

and they found a priceless object!

Austin found a map, _____

_____ .

Austin followed the map, _____

_____ .

They entered a dark cave, _____

_____ .

They reached the spot marked with

the *X*, _____

_____ .

Austin wanted the treasure to be safe,

_____

_____ .

Your opinion matters! For the first four sentences, add your opinion in the first blank. Then support your opinion by adding a reason in the second blank.

For the last sentence, write your own topic in the first blank, your opinion in the second blank, and your reason in the third blank.

An example has been done for you.

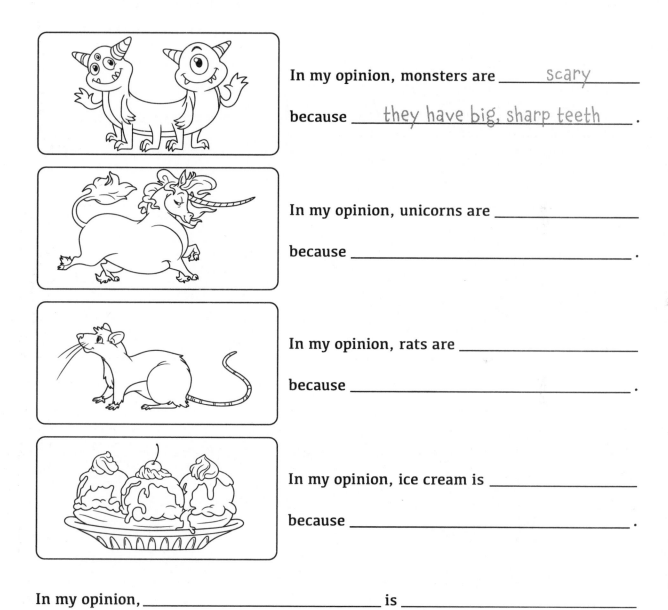

In my opinion, monsters are _____scary_____

because ____they have big, sharp teeth____.

In my opinion, unicorns are _____

because _____.

In my opinion, rats are _____

because _____.

In my opinion, ice cream is _____

because _____.

In my opinion, _____ is _____

because _____.

Look at the picture. Think about ways to conserve natural resources. Finish each sentence.

1. I recycle so that _____.

2. I save energy by _____.

3. I save water by _____.

Sentence Writing
Homographs

Look at the two pictures for each homograph. Write a sentence for each picture.
Use the homographs in the sentences.

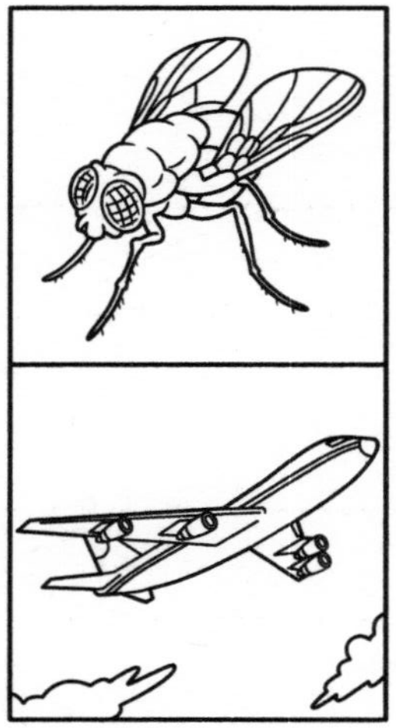

fly

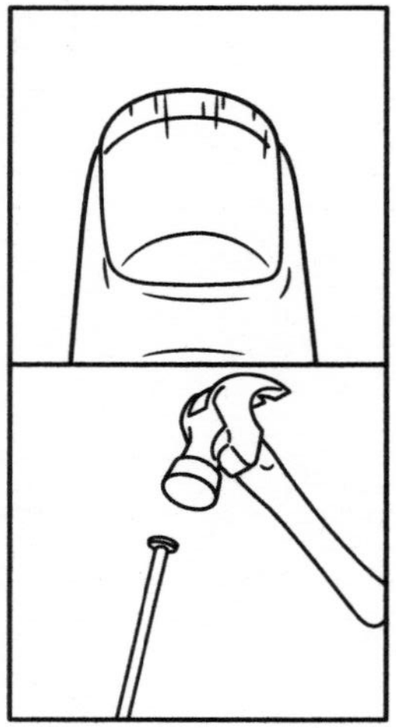

nail

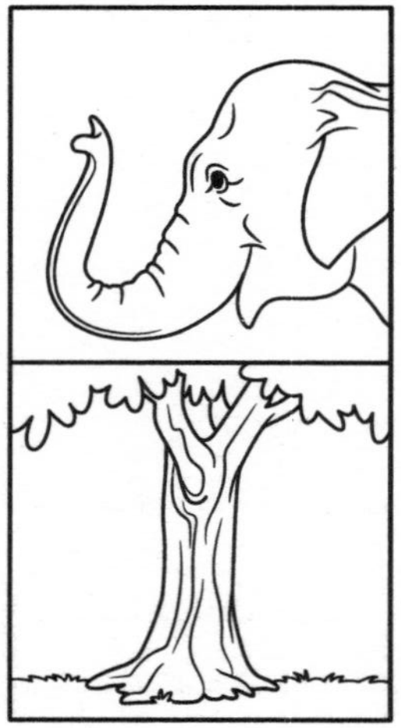

trunk

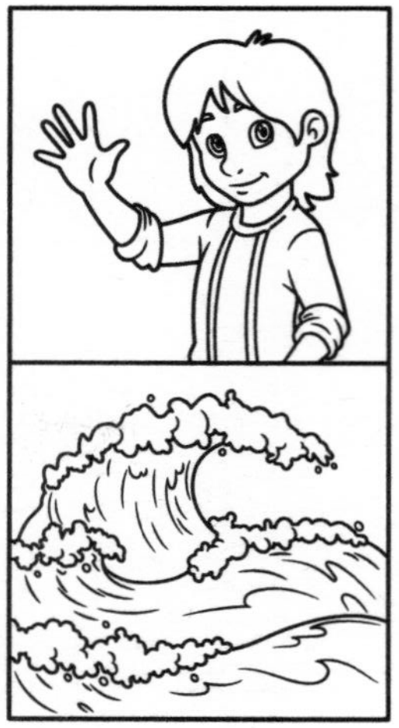

wave

Look at the picture. Finish each compound sentence to tell what is happening in the picture.

1.

King Richard wanted to have a feast, so he

_____.

2.

He couldn't decide if he should have sandwiches,

or if he _____.

3.

He tried one of each, but he _____

_____.

4.

The king canceled the feast, and he _____

_____.

Sentence Writing
Predicates: Grammar Kingdom

Look at the picture. Read the subject of the sentence. Write the predicate. The predicate tells what the subject is doing, did, or will do. Use the word box to help you.

leap down the street	dance in the fountain	sits on the king's crown	loves his bass

1. The parrot _____

2. The children _____

3. The knights _____

4. The musician _____

Amelia wants to write an informational text about dung beetles.
Fill in the blanks to tell what she is doing to plan her text.

1.

Amelia is _____
(brainstorming, drafting)
about the topic.

2.

Amelia is finding more _____ .
(information, pictures)

3.

Amelia is choosing the _____ ideas.
(main, most)

4.

Amelia is adding _____ like
(text features, main ideas)
pictures and a timeline.

Now Amelia is ready to write!

Look at the picture. Read the predicate. Then write the subject of the sentence.

1.

_____ blew smoke and fire.

2.

_____ and _____ fought the dragon together.

Look at the pictures and read the compound sentence. Choose and write the conjunction that best completes the sentence.

1.

The king and prince were bored, _____ they went on an adventure.
(so, or)

2.

They weren't looking for a dragon, _____ they found one!
(but, so)

3.

Ogre Yogurt

Flavors
raspberry
banana
vanilla

Later, the king got raspberry yogurt, _____ the prince got banana yogurt.
(and, or)

4.

They found a lake where they could go swimming, _____ they could sail a boat.
(so, or)

Think of a way that you use math in your life. Draw a picture of it. Write about your picture.

I use math for lots of things! What do you use math for?

I use math to: _____

Draw yourself as an underwater explorer. Write a sentence about the picture.

Draw a picture that shows water in different states. Then write about your picture.

Look at the picture. Draw something else to go in it. Write a sentence about the picture. Use one of the words in the word box. Color the picture.

Word Box

went	saw	said	did	ran	sat

Fill in the blanks with your own words or use words from the Word Box. Read the story aloud to make sure it makes sense. Then draw a picture to go with the story.

Word Box

brave	calm	across the fields	a drink of	nearby	for his kindness
noble	caring	through the kingdom	a sip of	dark	for his helpfulness
white	nice	black	hot	quickly	very
large	warm	instantly	quite	wide	

A _____ knight rode his _____ horse _____.

They became _____ thirsty. Soon the pair reached a _____

lake, but it was frozen solid! Suddenly a dragon came out of a _____

cave. The knight was _____ scared. But the _____ dragon

breathed _____ fire onto the lake. The ice melted _____!

The knight thanked the dragon _____.

Read the sentence. Find the missing part of speech in the word box.
Write it on the line.

Word Box

| pretty | King Grammar | queen | duck | sweetly | on | castle | ran |

1. The messenger_____ from

(verb)

the_____ .

(noun)

2. The _____ walked _____

(noun)   (preposition)

the path.

3. The _____ wore a

(noun)

_____ dress.

(adjective)

4. The queen looked _____

(adverb)

at _____ .

(proper noun)

Look at the picture. Read the sentence. Look at the prepositions below the line. Write the correct word.

1. The messenger ran _____
   (from, to)

   the castle.

2. The king jumped _____
   (under, over)

   the fence.

3. The king rode _____
   (over, under)

   the branch.

4. The king stood _____ his horse.
   (to, on)

5. The king fell _____ his horse.
   (off, over)

Look at the pictures. Write a sentence about something you need. Write another sentence about something you want. Color the pictures.

I need food because _____

I want toys because _____

Before you read about a topic, think about what you already know. After you read, think about what you learned. Let's try it!

What do you already know about the rules at the library?

_____

_____

_____

Rules at the Library

Books in the library are there for everyone to enjoy. Always wash your hands before handling books, and never eat or drink around them. And remember not to write in books or bend their pages. Libraries are mostly quiet places, so you shouldn't talk on a cell phone in a library. If you are using headphones, keep the volume low.

What is something new that you learned about the rules at the library?

_____

_____

_____

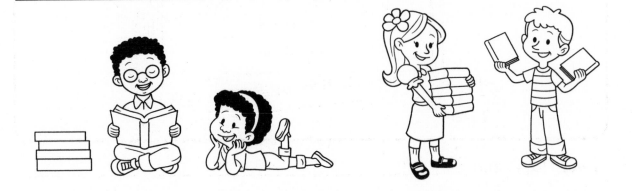

Write a sentence about the picture you see.

Write a sentence about the picture you see.

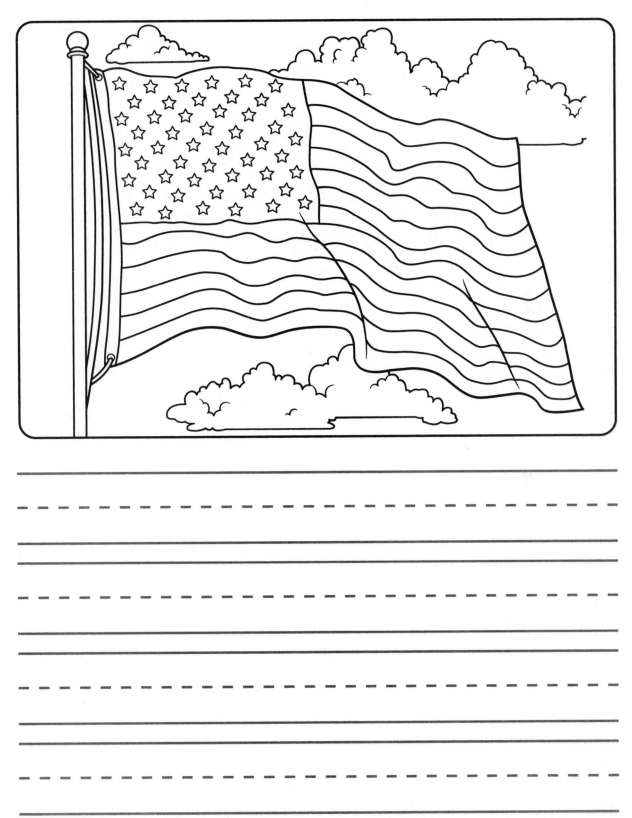

Write a sentence about the picture you see.

Think of a question you could ask about what you see in the picture, and write it down.

Write a sentence about the picture you see.

Write a sentence about the picture you see.

Write a sentence about the picture you see.

Write a sentence about the picture you see.

Write a sentence about the picture you see.

Write a sentence about the picture you see.

Write a sentence about the picture you see.

Write a sentence about the picture you see.

Write a sentence about the picture you see.

Write a sentence about the picture you see.
Use describing words in the sentence.

Write a sentence about the picture you see.

Look at the picture. Write about how this animal's body parts help it stay alive. Then color the picture.

Why is the water falling? Write a sentence about it.

AWESOME!

Great!

ABC Mouse

WOW!

Incredible!

Good job!

1-2-3 Mouse

Super job!

Nice going!

Well done!

Do-Re-Mi Mouse

TERRIFIC!

Very nice!

FANTASTIC!

You got it!

Yes!

Good!

AWESOME JOB!

SUPER!

Way to go!

NICE JOB!

Great job!

WONDERFUL!

Excellent!